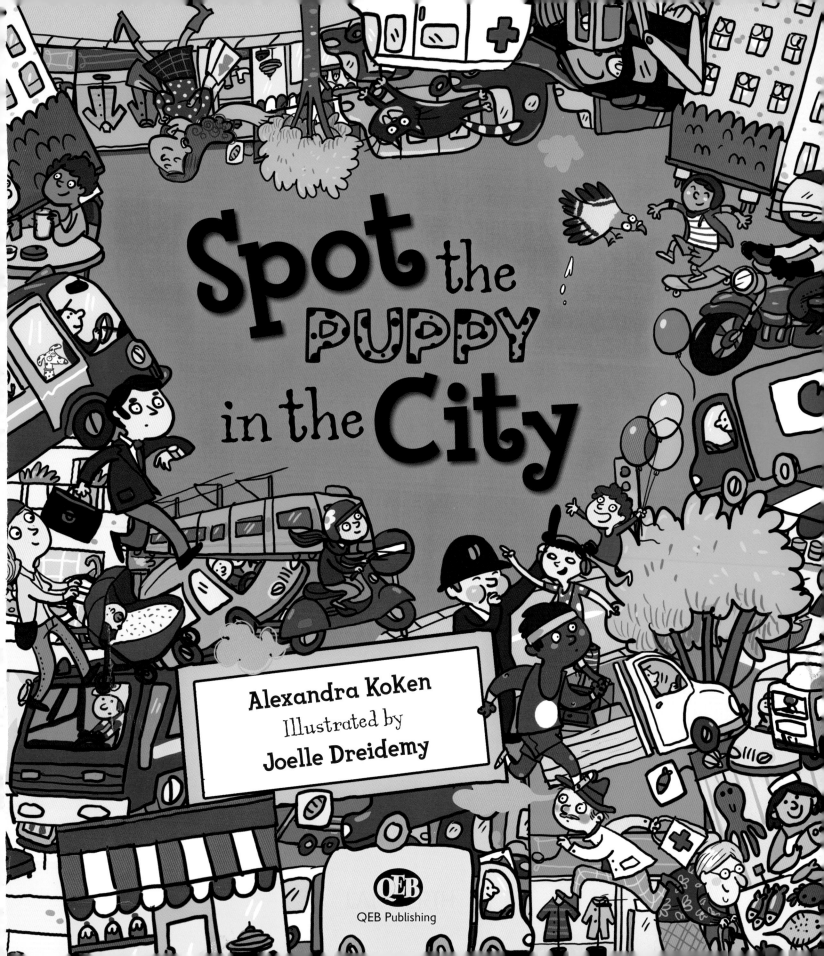

# Spot the PUPPY in the City

Alexandra Koken

Illustrated by

Joelle Dreidemy

QEB Publishing

Shopping Mall

Airport

Rush Hour

Train Station

Park

Fire Station

This puppy is hiding inside the book. Can you find him in every scene?

More people live in Tokyo, Japan, than in any other city in the world.

Can you spot these things?

banana skin · bucket · salad · clock · ax

Fire engines have sirens and flashing lights so people know they are coming.

Can you spot these things?

stripy kite · teddy bear · basket

lily pad · trash can · ice cream

The longest ever traffic jam was almost as long as 17 soccer fields.

The world's biggest
shopping mall
is in Dubai, UAE, and
has 1,200 stores!

Millions of people live close together in big cities.

Can you spot these things?

baseball cap shoe Triceratops notebook sign

# More to Spot

Go back and find these scenes in the book!

Did you find me?

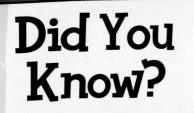

# Did You Know?

One of the busiest airports is in Atlanta, Georgia. One million planes take off from there every year.

In 1935, a man rode a bicycle around the world. He used seven sets of tires.

The first department store opened in 1734.

The biggest T-rex skeleton is called "Sue," and is kept in a museum in Chicago, Illinois.

The fastest road car can go 267 miles per hour (430 kmh). That's almost four times as fast as a cheetah!

# More City Fun!

### City Visit

There are lots of great things to see in every city! Ask an adult to take you to a city near you, and visit some of the places in this book: a park, a museum, or maybe a train station.

## Hide-and-Seek

Choose a stuffed animal that you can hide around your home for a friend or family member to spot, just like the puppy in this book! You could hide other objects and make a list of things to find.

### Dream City

Draw your very own dream city. You can add anything you want! Is there a park? Or maybe a sports stadium? What would the buildings look like? Once you are happy with your sketch, you can color it in and display it on your wall.

## Apartment Life

Using several different boxes stacked and glued together, make a block of houses like the ones in this book. Each box is a different apartment where people live. Fill it with toy furniture and people, or make your own. You can rearrange them whenever you like!

Designer: Krina Patel
Managing Editor: Victoria Garrard
Design Manager: Anna Lubecka

Copyright © QEB Publishing, Inc. 2013

First published in the United States by
QEB Publishing, Inc.
3 Wrigley, Suite A
Irvine, CA 92618

www.qed-publishing.co.uk

A CIP record for this book is available from the Library of Congress.

ISBN 978 1 60992 458 4

Printed in China